Fundamental

SOFTBALL

Coach Fred Wroge and the
following athletes were
photographed for this book:
    Tamara Anderson,
    Molly Chirico,
    Rachael Ekholm,
    Kathryn Hafertepe,
    Colleen Hinz,
    Dupe Omoyayi,
    Tripper Teslow,
    Katie Wells,
    Katie White,
    Leah Zarn.

Fundamental
SOFTBALL

Kristin Wolden Nitz

Photographs by Andy King

Lerner Publications Company
Minneapolis

7588775

To Kurt Nitz

Library of Congress Cataloging-in-Publication Data

Nitz, Kristin Wolden.
    Fundamental Softball / Kristin Wolden Nitz ; photographs by Andy King.
        p. cm.—(Fundamental sports)
    Includes bibliographical references and index.
    Summary: Introduces the history, equipment, skills, and strategies of softball.
    ISBN 0-8225-3460-6 (alk. paper)
    1. Softball—Juvenile literature. [1. Softball.] I. King, Andy, ill. II. Title. III. Series.
GV881.N58 1997
796.357'8—dc20   96-34258

Manufactured in the United States of America
1 2 3 4 5 6 – JR – 02 01 00 99 98 97

The Fundamental Sports series was conceptualized by editor Julie Jensen, designed by graphic artist Michael Tacheny, and composed on a Macintosh computer by Robert Mauzy. The Fundamental Sports series was designed in conjunction with the Beginning Sports series to offer young athletes a basic understanding of various sports at two reading levels.

Photo Acknowledgments
Photographs are reproduced with the permission of: p. 8, The Hennepin County Historical Society; pp. 9, 51, ALLSPORT/Jamie Squire; pp. 10, 16 (both) © Peter Ford; p. 11, Photo courtesy of Sports Vision 20/20.
Diagrams and artwork by Laura Westlund.

Contents

How This Game Got Started

Baseball may have the title of America's game, but softball is the game that Americans play. Each summer, more than 42 million people head to fields around the country. Of that number, some play only at an occasional picnic. About 4 million diehards play in six or more tournaments a year. The field of play ranges from backyards and parks to stadiums filled with cheering fans.

Historians trace the origin of softball back to Thanksgiving Day in 1887. A group of young men spent their holiday at Chicago's Farragut Boat Club, following the progress of the Harvard-Yale football game—one telegram at a time. Tension grew. Bets were made. Yale won. In the celebration that followed, an excited Yale booster threw a boxing glove at the Harvard group. A Harvard backer swung at the glove with a stick and sent it sailing back over the pitcher's head. George Hancock, who had been watching the horseplay, suggested that they play ball. He used the

7

glove's laces to tie it into a lumpy sphere and then drew the base paths on the gym floor with chalk.

In the chaotic hour that followed, the teams scored 80 runs between them. The event might have become nothing more than a pleasant memory except that George Hancock felt that they were onto something. He offered to write down a set of rules and provide a ball that wouldn't break any windows if his friends would stop by the boathouse on Saturday nights. By the end of that winter, *Indoor Base Ball* was being played all over Chicago.

While Hancock's game could be played either inside or out, a Minnesota fireman named Lewis Rober often gets the credit for moving the game outdoors. In 1895, he set up a field in the vacant lot outside his firehouse so that his men could get some exercise while waiting for an alarm. Rober's game had several advantages over baseball. It could be played on a smaller field since the ball couldn't travel as far. A full game could be completed in an hour instead of three. And that hour was packed with plenty of offense. The game spread to other firehouses.

Lewis Rober, a firefighter in Minnesota, refined the game of softball and took it outdoors.

Leagues were formed. Sometimes 3,000 spectators would attend the games. The competition grew so fierce that family members playing on different teams stopped speaking to each other during the season. The game became known as *kitten ball,* after Rober's first team—the Kittens.

Across the nation, different forms of the game evolved. Each region developed a set of rules and equipment requirements. The ball's size varied from 10 to 20 inches in circumference. The amusing, often insulting, names of the game ranged from *mush ball* and *pumpkin ball* to *sissy ball.* The last name was a complaint that softball was no longer for men only.

During much of the nineteenth century, the only games considered proper for women were noncontact sports like croquet, tennis, and badminton. The squishy ball, shorter field, and the nonviolent appearance of kitten ball gave women the opportunity to pick up a bat. But contrary to the illusions of some, women didn't trot gently around the bases. By 1926, when the term *softball* first began to be used, women were playing a highly competitive sport resembling the modern fast-paced college game.

The Chicago World's Fair of 1933 hosted the first national softball tournament for both women and men. More than 350,000 people attended the playoffs over the course of three days. The spectators then took softball home with them. Interest in the game spread across the nation. Leo Fischer, a reporter who organized and wrote about the world's fair tourney, helped to

Dot Richardson played shortstop for the 1996 U.S. gold-medal softball team.

Softball Surgeon

Many athletes have to undergo arthroscopic surgery for injuries. The shortstop for the 1996 Olympic softball team knows how to perform the procedure. Most surgical residents head straight to their beds after a long shift. Instead, Dot Richardson heads for her treadmill. It's not easy having two great loves.

Dot, who is in medical school, put her passion for medicine on hold a year to train fulltime for the 1996 Olympics in Atlanta. She's no stranger to international competition after playing on three Pan Am Games teams and in three International Federation world championships. But she says there's something special about representing her country in the Olympics.

Dot started in baseball but switched to softball by the age of 10. She jumped directly into a women's softball league. Three years later, she became the youngest player to join the national Women's Major Fast Pitch League. Since then, she has won seven Golden Glove awards, and is considered the best female shortstop ever.

People of all ages all over the world play softball for fun and exercise.

found the Amateur Softball Association (ASA) in the fall of the same year. The ASA started setting standards for rules and equipment.

Variations still abound. Some are officially recognized. Others are not. In Chicago, the cradle of softball, *Windy City* or *cabbage ball* is played with a 16-inch ball and without gloves. In Maine and Alaska, people play in the snow. In Washington and Idaho, some teams take snowball one step further and strap on a pair of snowshoes. At the opposite extreme, Californians developed a form to be played in the sand called *Over the Line*. OTL players don't use gloves, and they don't run the bases. These versions of the game are popular in their regions, but fast-pitch and slow-pitch softball dominate the game nationwide.

The best fast-pitch players can hurl the ball so that it crosses the plate with speeds above that of a Major League Baseball pitcher's fastball. They can put **stuff** on the ball so that it rises, drops, or curves as it approaches the plate. As in baseball, fast-pitch tends to be a low-scoring game. It's a duel between the pitcher and the batter.

Slow-pitch is a true team game. Everybody hits. Everybody fields. The pitcher's job is to lob the ball across the plate. The defense makes the outs. Slow-pitch has been played by people in their 70s and 80s. The difficulty in hitting a pitch with a high **arc** shouldn't be underestimated. Few things are more amusing to a slow-pitch player than watching a cocky fast-pitch player swing and miss the ball.

The ASA crowns national champions in both fast-pitch and slow-pitch, but fast-pitch dominates international competition. Softball has been played at the international level since the 1960s, but it took another 30 years for the game to arrive as a medal sport at the 1996 Summer Olympic Games.

Special Rules for Special Players

The game is called Beep Baseball, but it is clearly an ingenious adaptation of softball for visually impaired athletes. The ball has a circumference of 16 inches. It is pitched underhand.

Sighted players pitch and catch for their teammates. The pitcher shouts "Ready" as the pitch leaves the fingers and then "Ball" at the moment the batter should swing. A beeping telephone installed in the center of the ball gives the player added information about the ball's position. It requires many hours of working together to perfect the teamwork between pitcher and batter.

Once a batter makes contact, a scorekeeper will hit a button that starts one of two 4-foot pylons buzzing. These bases are located along the first and third base lines. The batter will wait to hear which pylon is buzzing before running full speed in the direction of the sound. Meanwhile, the fielders are listening intently so they can field the beeping ball. If the batter can make it to the base before one of six fielders "captures" the ball, a run is scored. Otherwise, the runner is out.

Beep ball is played in cities and camps around the nation and in other countries.

Chapter 2

THE BASICS

Since the 1930s, the Amateur Softball Association has promoted softball as a sport for everyone. Young players begin by hitting balls off a tee. At the next level, the batter faces a pitcher. Soon, the pitches get faster. While some players continue the climb through the high school and college ranks, others head into the recreational leagues. The term "recreational" should not be confused with noncompetitive. These players play with a high level of intensity even as they're having fun. After the game, they discuss each play with a thoroughness that sportscasters reserve for championships.

Each league and every level has its own peculiarities and special rules. But despite small differences in equipment and field size, the game is instantly recognizable as softball.

The pitcher's rubber

The batter's boxes on either side of home plate

The Field of Play

The field is really a square resting on one of its angles, which is why it is often referred to as a *diamond*. Home plate, where the batter stands, is the base of the diamond. First base is to the right of home, second base is directly across from home, and third base is to the left. The bases are 55 to 65 feet apart, depending on the type of game. The raked dirt around the bases is called the infield. The grassy region beyond is the outfield.

The **pitcher's rubber** lies 35 to 50 feet from home plate in a direct line between second base and home. Unlike baseball, softball does not have a mound or a grass infield.

Foul lines run from the pointed back of home plate, along the outer edges of first and third base and out to the fence. On some fields, the lines are marked with chalk. On others, the umpires use a pole, their unbiased judgment, eaglelike eyesight, and a little imagination to make the call. A ball landing between those two lines is in fair territory. A ball that first hits the ground outside those lines is considered a **foul ball**. A ball that hits the ground in fair territory and rolls across the foul lines before reaching first or third base is also a foul ball.

The two rectangles on either side of home plate are the batter's boxes. The areas marked in chalk to the left of third base and the right of first base are coaching boxes. This is where the coaches stand when their team is batting.

Distances Table

Fast-pitch

Division	Distance between bases	Distance from pitcher's rubber to home plate
ages 10 and under	55'	35'
girls 12 and under	60'	35'
boys 12 and under	60'	40'
girls 18 and under	60'	40'
boys 18 and under	60'	46'
Adult women	60'	40'
Adult men	60'	46'

Slow-pitch

Division	Distance between bases	Distance from pitcher's rubber to home plate
ages 10 and under	55'	35'
girls 12 and under	60'	40'
girls 14 and under	65'	46'
girls 18 and under	65'	50'
boys 12 and under	60'	40'
boys 14 and under	65'	46'
boys 18 and under	65'	50'
Adult	65'	50'

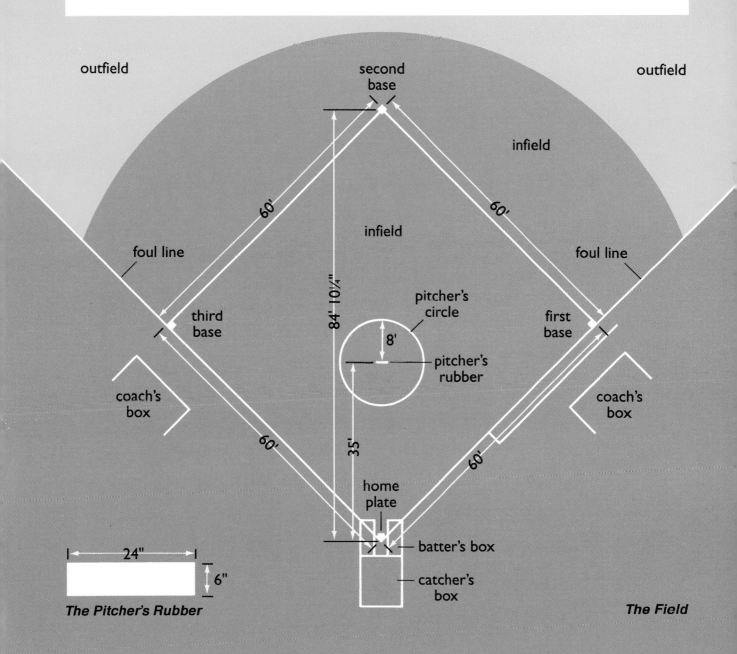

The Pitcher's Rubber

The Field

Equipment

● *The Ball*

There's nothing soft about softballs. Inside the cowhide or synthetic cover, yarn is tightly wound around a cork, rubber, or fiber center. The three parts of a softball are the core, the winding, and the cover. The 12-inch ball has an interior core measuring three and a half inches in diameter. The winding is about 1/16th of an inch thick. Cotton-polyester yarn is wrapped around the core before being dipped into a special solution to hold the thread in place. The cover is also about 1/16th of an inch thick. It is cemented to the winding and hand stitched.

The 12-inch circumference is double the circumference of a baseball and, at 7 ounces, a softball weighs slightly more than a baseball. While the 12-inch ball is the standard, balls come in many different sizes and colors. Youth leagues often use an 11-inch ball. Boxes of 16-inch balls are sent to Chicago for cabbage ball. The Over the Line players demand kapok balls with rubber covers. Kapok's silky fiber core becomes mushy during the game. Neon orange cork balls are used in the snow. Other "softies" are still made for the indoor game.

Because of their core construction and increased wind resistance, softballs don't fly as far as baseballs. That is why the distance from home plate to the outer fence is a little more than half that of a baseball park.

● *The Glove*

Gloves should be chosen with care to make sure the **pocket** between the thumb and forefinger is large enough to catch the ball. Gloves actually improve with each season because the leather becomes more flexible with use. A glove can be broken in faster by rubbing it with a conditioner. Between games and practices, many players leave a ball in the pocket and tie it shut.

A catcher's mitt, above, is bigger and doesn't have the individual finger spaces that a fielder's glove, below, does.

Batting helmets, at left, are hard plastic foam-lined hats that protect players while they're batting and running. Bats, at right, come in many sizes and colors.

● *The Bat*

Each bat has a handle, a barrel, and a knob. Players grip the bat on the taped handle and try to hit the ball with the thicker barrel. The main function of the knob is to keep the bat from slipping out of the batter's hands. Bats are made of wood or aluminum. Aluminum bats are lighter and last longer.

A team's equipment bag will have a variety of bats. The bigger bats may carry nicknames like "Bleacher-reacher," but it's more important to pick a bat light enough to accelerate off your shoulder. The faster you swing, the more power you can transfer to the ball. Grip the bat by the knob with your weaker arm. Hold the bat straight out in front of you. If the bat sags down, try a lighter bat.

● Other Equipment

Special shoes with rubber cleats can provide increased traction, but many people feel more comfortable with a running shoe or court shoe. Softball players usually wear loose, comfortable clothes to practice. Jeans or sweats can save wear and tear on legs. Game uniforms can vary from a T-shirt and shorts to a team jersey and short pants called knickers. No jewelry is allowed. Rings can be especially dangerous. A jammed finger can swell up so rapidly that a doctor must cut off the ring to restore circulation.

Batters and runners must wear batting helmets to prevent head injuries. The catcher must have a face mask, helmet, chest protector, and shin guards.

A catcher must wear protective gear in case he or she is hit by a ball or an incoming runner.

Shoes with cleats help players keep their footing on slippery outfield grass.

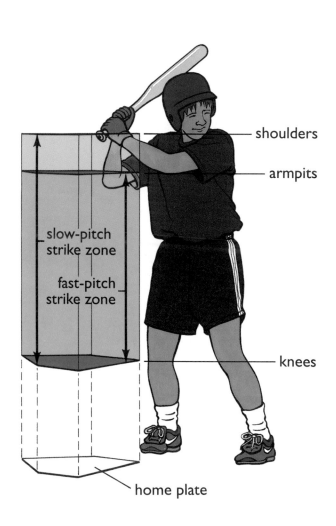

shoulders

armpits

slow-pitch
strike zone

fast-pitch
strike zone

knees

home plate

Strike Zones

The Rules

The batter steps into one of the chalked batter's boxes on either side of home plate. The pitcher tries to throw the ball through the batter's **strike zone** using an underhand motion. In fast-pitch, the strike zone is the space over the plate that ranges from the batter's knees to the armpits. In slow-pitch, the zone continues up to the shoulders.

The batter does not have to swing at the pitch. If the batter doesn't swing and the ball doesn't pass through the strike zone, the umpire will call a **ball**. The umpire will call a **strike** if the batter doesn't swing at a pitch in the strike zone. A batter can also get a strike by swinging at the ball and missing, or by hitting the ball into foul territory. A batter remains at the plate until hitting a ball into fair territory, taking four balls for a **walk** to first base, or getting three strikes for an **out**. If the **count** is already at two strikes, a foul ball will not be called a strike unless it's a "three fouls and you're out" league.

If the batter hits a fair ball, the defenders can make a **force-out** by throwing the ball to first base before the runner gets there. The umpire will call the runner out as long as the defensive player has control of the ball and a foot on the bag. If another runner is already on base, the defense will often choose to pick off the lead runner. It's important to remember that if the lead runner doesn't have to run, a fielder must **tag** the runner to get an out. For example, a runner on second doesn't have to go to third if first base is empty. If the runner heads to third, the person playing third will place the ball in his or her glove and touch the runner with it to get the runner out. The defense can also tag an offensive player who over-runs second or third base.

The defense can also put the batter out by catching a fair or foul ball before it hits the ground. When that happens, all runners on base must **tag up**, that is they must be touching their original base until the ball is caught. When a **fly ball** is hit deep into the outfield, a runner may tag up and then run to the next base. Since the runner doesn't have to run, he or she must be tagged out.

The offense scores a run when a person makes it all the way around the bases without being tagged or forced out. Each team bats until the defense makes three outs. An inning is completed when both teams have batted. The visiting team bats first. This is called the *top* of the inning. The home team bats second, or in the *bottom* of the inning. Softball games last seven innings unless there is a tie or the game is rained out. The team with the most runs wins.

Chapter 3

FIELDING AND THROWING

Softball has a long list of rules and special strategies that must be learned to play the game effectively. On defense, it's important to know where to make the throw and whether the runner should be tagged or if just having a foot on the base will do. But the mechanics can be broken down into two parts: stopping the ball and effectively sending it to the right place—otherwise known as fielding and throwing.

Fielding

● *Fly Balls*

The secret to catching a fly ball is to watch it from the instant it leaves the bat until it smacks into the glove. Sprint toward the area where you think the ball will come down. As you run, repeatedly tell your teammates that you've got it. Even if you misjudge the ball and it winds up in someone else's territory, the catch is yours to make.

Catching a tennis ball with your bare hands is a good way to practice.

Catching the Ball

There are two important principles to remember when catching the ball. The first may sound too basic to even be mentioned, but even people playing at a very advanced level make this mistake. You have to catch the ball before you can make the play. On countless occasions, players have bobbled the ball because they're thinking about making the tag instead of trapping the ball first.

The second principle sounds equally basic: Use two hands when catching the ball. That may sound like a rule for beginners, but it's not. Trapping the ball with your bare hand will keep it from ricocheting out. And with your hand already in position, you can quickly get rid of the ball.

Doing the Diamond

The diamond drill can help with speed, agility, and conditioning. Begin with your feet shoulder width apart. Jump so that your right foot lands at the top of the diamond while your left foot lands on the bottom. Return to the starting point, and then repeat the first motion except that your feet go to the opposite points of the diamond. Begin slowly to master the steps and then go faster and faster until you've reached full speed. Rest for a few seconds and then do the diamond drill again.

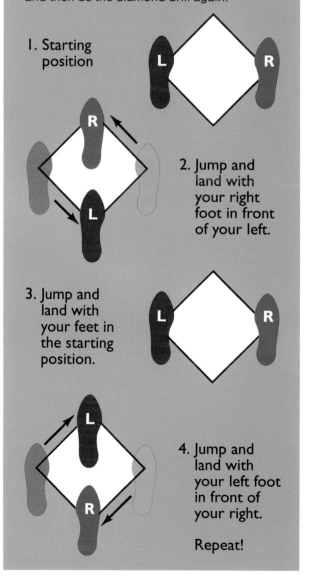

1. Starting position

2. Jump and land with your right foot in front of your left.

3. Jump and land with your feet in the starting position.

4. Jump and land with your left foot in front of your right.

Repeat!

Molly, below, demonstrates how to catch a fly ball. She gets under the ball and positions her glove above her eyes so that its fingers are pointing up. This gives Molly a good view of the ball and shields her eyes from the sun's glare. As the ball thuds into the pocket, she covers, or traps, the ball with her other hand.

When a ball is driven deep into the outfield, Rachael, above, doesn't back-pedal. Instead, she turns and runs while watching the ball over her left shoulder. She catches the ball as she would a football pass.

It's important for a fielder to get under a fly ball. It's essential to get in front of a **ground ball.**

● *Ground Balls*

Since ground balls can be unpredictable, fielders must be ready to block the ball with their bodies. If the ball strikes a rock or an uneven piece of ground, it can take a **bad hop** in an unexpected direction.

As Tripper, at left, takes infield practice, he waits in the ready position. His feet are wide apart, his knees bent, his shoulders ahead of his hips, and his glove is down and open.

When a grounder bounces across the infield, Tripper moves in front of the ball. As he sets up to make the catch, the tip of his glove touches the ground so the ball won't roll through his legs. Tripper watches the ball until it enters his glove. Then he quickly traps the ball with his bare hand to keep it from bouncing out.

If the ball is rolling slowly, charge toward it, as Kathy does on the next page. Not only will she reach the ball faster, but also her throw will be shorter. The time saved in charging a ground ball can make the difference between a runner being safe or out.

Kathy gets in front of the ball to block it with her body. She knows if the ball gets past her, the runners will get extra bases. Like Tripper, she fixes her eye on the ball until it enters her glove and then covers the ball with her throwing hand.

Off the Wall

You can work on your fielding even on days when you don't have anyone to play catch with you. Throw a tennis ball against a wall or sturdy garage door. Change the angle, height, and speed of your throw so you can practice stopping many kinds of grounders.

● *Line Drives*

A flat, hard-hit **line drive** doesn't leave a fielder much time to react. One of the toughest types to catch is when the ball is hit directly at the body.

In the photo at left, the line drive is above Kathy's waistline, so she catches the ball with her fingers and glove pointing up. In the photo below, she catches a zinger below the belt with her fingers pointing down.

On plays like this, things happen so fast that there isn't much time to think. That's why Kathy thinks through all of her options before the batter even steps up to the plate. Then she can focus on making a good throw to the right base.

Warmups

Players don't just walk onto the field and start charging ground balls and throwing as hard as they can. To prevent injuries, it's important to warm up first. Many teams begin by jogging around the outside of the softball field to loosen up and get extra blood flowing to their muscles. This is often followed by a series of stretching exercises. There are three things to remember while stretching.

1. Never stretch to the point of pain.
2. Don't hold your breath. Inhale and exhale normally.
3. Stretch both sides of the body equally.

Finally, be sure to warm up your throwing arm. Sometimes, players will play catch on their knees. Not only is this a good way to warm up your arm, but it's also a good way to focus on the upper body motion of the overhand and snap throws.

Throwing

People talk about fielders having "good arms," but a fielder's whole body should be involved in generating power for a long throw. The proper movement of the ball-hand leg gives power to the throwing arm above it. There are several different techniques for throwing the ball. Each one has its own application. Each one begins with a good grip.

Hold the ball with your fingertips, not in your palm. Try placing your middle finger and forefinger where the seams come together. Then hold your thumb underneath the ball to form an imaginary triangle passing through the softball.

● *Overhand*

Outfielders use the overhand throw to return the ball to the infield. After Colleen, below, makes the catch, she faces her target and takes a short step forward with her ball-hand leg. As her glove-hand foot moves forward, her glove shoulder and hip point to her target. At the same time, her throwing arm is back with the wrist cocked.

As her arm comes forward, her elbow passes her ear. Colleen shifts her weight forward to her glove-hand foot as she releases the ball. On the follow-through, her throwing hand finishes just above her knee.

Team Player

Have you ever heard someone say, "What a team player!" That's a high compliment for a softball player, or any athlete. What it means is that player puts the good of the team ahead of personal preferences or desires.

Being a team player can mean taking care of yourself so that you're always ready to play. That means eating right, getting enough rest, and stretching before you throw or practice. It's a lot of fun to sit in the dugout with your teammates while waiting to bat. It's not so much fun to be stuck in the dugout because you're injured.

Being a team player also means listening to your coach. Each coach does things in his or her own way. That means that what your coach last year did might not be what this year's coach does. A team player knows how to adjust to the coach's style. No coach likes to hear, "But Coach Johnson didn't do it that way."

Doing the Crow Hop

On a deep throw from the outfield, some players add an extra short step, called a crow hop. They step with their ball-hand foot before making a regular overhand throw. This move protects the arm and increases a player's throwing range.

Rachael demonstrates the crow hop. First, she fields the ball. She faces her target and takes a short step forward with her ball-hand leg.

Rachael hops on her ball-hand leg to add momentum. Her glove-hand shoulder and hip point to her target. She brings her throwing arm back with the wrist cocked.

As her arm comes forward, Rachael shifts her weight forward to her glove-hand foot as she releases the ball in front of her body. On the follow-through, her throwing hand finishes above her knee.

● *Sidearm*

In addition to the overhand throw, in-fielders use the sidearm throw. The motion for the sidearm throw is similar to skipping a stone on a lake. Molly is making a sidearm throw in the photos on this page. Notice that Molly's fore-arm is parallel to the ground, and follows through across her body. This throw saves time since Molly doesn't have to bring her arm all the way back. Molly can also use this throw when she is off balance.

● Snap throw

Snap throws are valuable in a rundown when a runner is trapped between bases. Below, Kathy's hand begins by her ear and ends with her arm at shoulder height and parallel to the ground.

● Underhand

A player can deliver the ball quickly from a crouch with an underhand throw. Since Dupe is only a few feet from the base, she gently tosses the ball so her teammate can catch it. She

is careful that the ball doesn't spin off her fingers and over her teammate's head. Of course, the most important use for the underhand throw in softball is in pitching.

Chapter 4

PITCHING

Good pitching technique requires much more than an underhand toss in the general direction of the batter. Pitching takes consistency, control, and concentration. It can be a long, long game when the pitcher can't find the plate.

Good pitchers coordinate their footwork with the release of the ball to develop a rhythm. They also develop mental and emotional strength. They can shake it off after walking a batter or allowing a home run.

Both slow- and fast-pitch pitchers need the same kind of mental tough-

ness, but the rules of each game make the style of delivery very different. In slow-pitch softball, the ball's arc must range from a minimum of 3 feet from the point of release to a maximum of 12 feet from the ground. An umpire will warn a pitcher only once about excessive speed. After that, the umpire will remove the pitcher from the game. In sharp contrast, the fast-pitch ball cannot have an arc of more than 3 feet. A pitch's speed is limited only by the strength and skill of the pitcher and the laws of physics.

Pitching Arcs

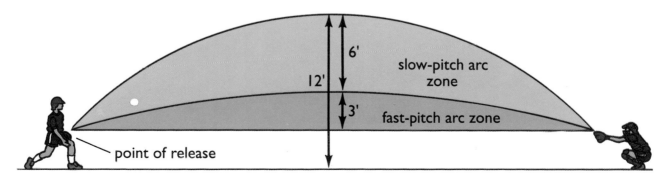

6'

12'

slow-pitch arc zone

3'

fast-pitch arc zone

point of release

Slow-Pitch Delivery

To pitch for a slow-pitch game, Kathy begins with her ball-hand foot on the pitcher's rubber and her other foot back. Her front foot cannot leave the pitcher's rubber until she releases the ball. She grips the ball with her fingers. She holds the ball behind her glove and in front of her chest for no less than two seconds. Then she swings her arm back gently until the ball is no more than hip high. Kathy steps forward as

she swings her arm forward and releases the ball just past her hip. She immediately jumps back and gets ready to field. The batter can return the ball to the pitcher with blistering speed.

The pitcher can keep the batter guessing by varying the arc on the throw. It may seem strange, but with the proper arc, the ball can pass through the strike zone and hit the back of the plate for a strike.

Pitching Warmup

Whether you're practicing in your backyard or getting ready for a game, it is important to warm up your arm properly. Begin with running. On a cool day, you should wear a jacket to keep the heat you generate near your arm. Next, play catch gently, tossing the ball both underhand and overhand. This stretches muscles in the back, shoulder, and forearm.

Once you begin the pitching motion, make sure that you're the regulation distance away from your catcher. Start at half speed and accelerate slowly until you're throwing what you'd send to a batter. Do this for each pitch in your arsenal. When that's complete, you can start mixing them up as in a game situation.

Fast-Pitch Delivery

There are two types of deliveries in fast-pitch: the slingshot and the windmill. The slingshot resembles a slow-pitch delivery, except there's nothing gentle about it. The arm is drawn back slowly before being whipped forward. The windmill is more popular because of the higher speeds it can generate, but many pitchers master the slingshot first. The windmill got its name from old-fashioned trick pitches. Pitchers would rotate their arms a number of times to confuse the batters. Current rules allow only one revolution.

● *Slingshot*

In keeping with the rules, Rachael begins with both feet touching the pitcher's rubber, as shown in the photo at left. Her ball-hand heel rests on top of the rubber while the toe of her other foot presses against the back of the rubber.

On the next page, Rachael curves her fingers around the ball in a two- or three-fingered grip. In fast-pitch, the placement of the pitcher's fingers will affect the movement of the ball as it travels across the plate. Rachael's hands are down and in front of her body. She hides her grip in her glove for no less than one second.

Rachael brings the ball out of her glove. As she rotates her arm back, she steps forward with her glove-hand foot. By the time the ball reaches its highest point above and behind her head, her striding leg is fully extended.

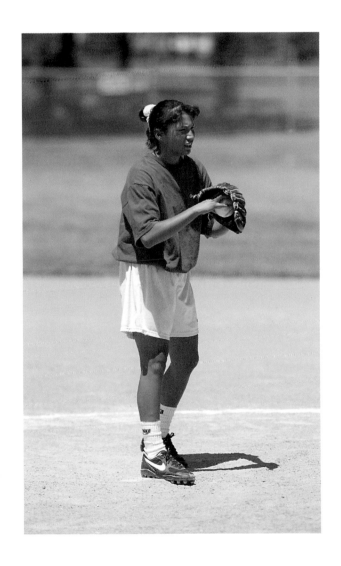

This side view shows how high above her head Rachael brings the ball during the slingshot.

But Rachael keeps all of her weight back until she whips her arm forward in a plane parallel to her body. She plants her foot an instant before the release. Her wrist snaps forward, adding speed and spin to the ball as it leaves her fingertips. Rachael's back foot leaves the mound an instant later.

After the release, Rachael's arm con-

tinues to rotate upward in a smooth motion. The height of the hand on the follow-through depends on what is comfortable for the pitcher. Since the ball could come straight back at her, Rachael instantly gets into fielding position. To do that, she makes sure that her striding foot hits the ground pointing directly at the batter.

Leah's leg is fully extended. Once again, Leah keeps her weight back until passing this balance point to avoid throwing with just her arm. Leah snaps her wrist forward on the release as the ball passes her thigh. Her front foot hits the ground at the instant she releases the ball. Her back foot leaves the pitcher's rubber an instant later.

After the release, Leah's arm continues to rotate up in a smooth motion. Then she quickly steps forward into fielding position.

Some pitchers find that adding a pump motion to the windmill gives them better control. The ball and glove are brought up together to the chest or face so that the grip is still hidden. As both arms head back to the original ready position, the ball hand leaves the glove. At that point, the arm starts forward and concludes in the usual windmill delivery. The altered rhythm can baffle opposing batters.

This straight-ahead view shows Leah releasing the ball just as her hand passes her thigh.

The drop ball grip

The rise ball grip

The curveball grip

Stuff

An assortment of grips and ball rotations enables a pitcher to put stuff on the ball. Instead of traveling directly across the plate, these balls move sharply up, down, or to the side. The most common pitches are called, not surprisingly, the **rise ball, drop ball,** and **curveball.** A fourth pitch, called the **changeup,** is usually a slower drop or rise ball. The sudden decrease in speed and spin can fool hitters and make them swing ahead of the pitch. The key to a good change-of-pace pitch is to make the delivery look like every other pitch.

Several common grips are shown at left. Each pitcher modifies the basic form. For the drop ball, many pitchers use a two- or three-fingered grip. The fingers are placed evenly across the seams. The ball is released with a simple underhand motion. It spins towards the batter and drops suddenly as it approaches the plate. The faster the pitch, the more sharply the ball will drop. Batters will often hit grounders when they swing at a drop ball.

For the rise ball, the middle finger is bent. As the hand passes the leg, the wrist rotates toward the body. This rotation causes the ball to roll off the fingertips with back spin. The curveball is delivered in much the same way as the rise ball, but on the follow-through the arm should move across the body. Rising pitches often cause fly balls.

Developing stuff takes months or even years of practice. But merely being able to change the rotation of the ball can pay off right away by confusing the batter.

Hot Stuff

Lisa Fernandez, who was a pitcher on the gold medal-winning U.S. women's Olympic softball team in 1996, played her first game as a pitcher when she was eight years old. She walked 20 batters and her team lost the game 28–0. Instead of giving up, she decided that she would do better next time. She did. She continued to improve her game and ended her four college years at UCLA with a stunning record of 709 **strikeouts,** nine no-hitters, three perfect games, and an earned run average of 0.22. (An earned run occurs when the run is not the result of a defensive error, such as dropping a fly ball. To calculate an earned run average, divide the number of earned runs by the number of innings pitched, and then multiply by seven.)

Lisa was also a serious offensive threat. In her senior year, she had a .507 batting average, the best in the nation. With that devastating hitting and pitching combination, Fernandez led the Bruins to four Women's College World Series. They won NCAA championships twice and finished as runners-up on alternate years. Following graduation, Lisa played for the Raybestos Brakettes, which is one of the ASA's powerhouses, before leading the U.S. team to the gold.

HITTING AND RUNNING

After all the endless drills and fielding practice, everyone wants to take a turn at bat. There's nothing like connecting solidly with a pitch, beating a throw to first, or sliding under a tag. It's undeniably the most fun part of practice. Your teammates may be facing you in their oldest jeans and colorful T-shirts, but suddenly you can transport yourself to the league championships: "It's two outs in the bottom of the seventh. The score is tied with the go-ahead run on third...." But just as in fielding, throwing, and pitching, it's important to learn the right techniques for hitting, running, and sliding.

Hitting

● Grip

Just like throwing and pitching, hitting begins with the right grip. In the photo at right, Leah holds her hands together so that the hand knuckles of her top hand line up with the finger knuckles of her bottom hand. Some batters move their hands closer to the barrel, or choke up, on the bat for extra control as Leah has done in the photo to the far right.

On the left, Leah shows the regular way to grip a bat. On the right, she shows how to choke up on the bat. Players choke up when a pitcher is throwing very fast, the bat they're using is too heavy, or they want to have an exceptionally quick swing.

53

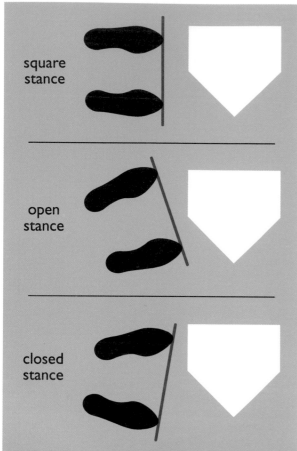

square stance

open stance

closed stance

High-Powered Footwork

*Beginning players are urged to begin with their feet in the parallel, or square, stance with both toes pointed directly at the plate. It's easier to fix any timing problems with the stride from that position. Later, some batters find they prefer the open stance where the front foot is farther away from the plate. On an inside pitch, they can **pull** a ball down the foul line on the same side of the plate that they're standing on. Other batters will try to hit across to the **opposite field** by taking a closed stance where the front foot is closer to the plate.*

Slow-pitch players can actually shift their stances while the ball is in the air. For example, if an inside pitch is on the way, the batter can shift to an open stance to hit it down the foul line. Fast-pitch batters don't have time for any adjustments to their stance once the ball leaves the pitcher's hand.

● *Stance*

Leah steps into the batter's box. She stands with her feet about shoulder width apart and her knees flexed. She cocks the bat back behind her ear halfway between the horizontal and the vertical. Her hands are even with her shoulders, and she holds her arms comfortably away from her body. She keeps her shoulders level and the bat off her shoulder. After taking a practice swing to make sure her bat can cover the entire plate, Leah watches the pitcher with her chin just above her front shoulder. Once the pitcher begins the delivery, Leah will focus on the ball.

● *Swing*

As the pitcher delivers, Leah shifts her weight to her back foot. Her shoulders rotate back slightly so that her swing doesn't begin from a dead stop. Her eyes are on the ball. Leah steps toward the pitcher with her front foot but does not shift her weight forward until she begins her forward swing. Leah's back hip follows the forward rotation of her hands, using her back foot as a pivot. She plants her front foot. Her arms are fully extended as she watches the ball down the barrel of the bat.

Curing Pop Ups

Few things are more frustrating than stepping up to the plate only to pop up the ball high over the infield. Popping up may have a number of causes. One possibility is that you are hitting under the ball instead of hitting it squarely. But, oddly enough, one of the first things you should check is your stride. Some players have been miraculously cured by taking a shorter stride and making sure that they end with their front leg straight rather than bent.

Practice Drills for Hitting

You may have left the tee-ball league behind, but hitting off a tee, as Colleen is above, can help your swing. Players at all levels benefit from this drill. Focus on one or two parts of your swing. For example, one day you may want to work on fully extending your arms and snapping your wrists. The next day, concentrate on your stride and shifting your weight forward at the proper time.

The soft toss drill Colleen and Dupe are doing below is another good one. Stand close to a fence and have a teammate or friend gently toss a ball toward you. Swing hard and hit the ball into the fence.

She snaps her wrists as the bat makes contact with the ball. Leah rolls her wrists over as she swings hard "through" the ball. She ends with her front leg straight and her back leg bent. Her hands finish near her front shoulder.

Sometimes a voice from the stands will yell "Wait until the ball crosses the plate." That classic phrase is one of the worst pieces of advice that a batter can take. On an outside pitch, the batter may have a prayer of connecting with the ball, but the time for hitting an inside pitch has already come and gone. To achieve full extension for the arms and maximum power, batters should connect with an inside pitch about three feet in front of the plate. When the ball comes right down the middle, the bat should make contact two feet in front of the plate. This is called "hitting the ball where it's pitched."

● Bunt

The ball bounces off the bat, rolls a few feet from home plate, and stops. There's a moment of confusion as two or more people converge on the ball. Batters who know how to **bunt** can cause this chaos deliberately.

In slow-pitch, a bunt is an automatic out. In fast-pitch, bunting is an offensive weapon. The bunt can be used when trying to make contact against a hard-throwing pitcher or to keep the infielders honest. Infielders have to respect players who can bunt well and they must play them close. Once the count reaches two strikes, many batters return to their normal swing. A foul bunt will count as the third strike.

The **sacrifice bunt** is a well-known method of advancing a runner. It's known as a sacrifice because the batter often will be thrown out at first base.

In the photos at right, Tripper demonstrates a sacrifice bunt. When the pitcher begins her windup, Tripper pivots to face her. The infielders are instantly alerted that Tripper intends to hit a sacrifice bunt, and the players at first and third charge toward the plate.

Tripper slides his top hand along the bat with his fingers on the bottom and his thumb on the top. In this position, he can cushion the ball's impact while protecting his fingers. He adjusts to the height of the pitch with his legs. Instead of swinging, Tripper lets the ball meet the underside of the bat and directs the ball into the dirt.

The **drag bunt** is used when the batter wants to reach first base safely. The basic form for the drag bunt resembles that of the sacrifice bunt. The biggest difference is in the timing. Molly, above, acts as though she will swing away, but then quickly shifts into the bunting stance while the ball is in the air. As she pushes the ball down one of the baselines, Molly is already on her way to first base. That head start can be the difference between getting on base and being thrown out.

Running the Bases

Intelligent, heads-up baserunning is important to the offense. Every player on base should know the count, the number of outs, and the score. All of these factors will dictate how aggressively a person can run the bases.

The runner should listen to the base coaches for information on whether to slide, come in standing up, or even try for another base. The base coaches will watch the ball for the runners.

The base coaches will also deliver the signal to steal, using a series of gestures. Before the game, the coach may tell the team that a nose scratch means steal, a shoulder touch means stay, and a chin rub means run on a wild throw. All the other motions are used to make sure the other team doesn't guess the code.

● Getting to First

At right, Dupe shows how to run to first. After connecting with the pitch, Dupe takes the first step with her back foot. Both right- and lefthanded players should take off in that way from home plate. It's effective because the player's weight has been shifted to the front foot during the swing.

Dupe doesn't stop to watch the ball. She pumps her arms like a sprinter and runs straight across the bag. Since players can overrun first base, there's no point in slowing down or trying to slide into first. The only time a runner may wish to slide is when the person playing first is drawn off the base and is looking to make the tag.

Dropped Third Strike Rule

In fast-pitch, three strikes doesn't always mean a quick trip back to the bench. If the catcher drops the third strike, the runner can try to beat the throw to first base if:
1. *First base is empty.*
2. *First base is occupied, but there are already two outs.*

This rule prevents the catcher from dropping the third strike on purpose to get two outs. So if you get that third strike, check to make sure that the catcher hasn't dropped the ball.

On an **extra-base hit,** below, Dupe veers out in a slight arc on the way to first. As she approaches the bag, she turns toward second and hits the inside corner with her foot.

She's careful to touch every base. If the umpire sees her miss a base, she will be called out.

● *Stealing*

Just as there is no bunting in slow-pitch, there isn't any stealing either. This makes sense because a runner could tear up a considerable distance to the next base as the ball made its leisurely way to the plate. In fast-pitch, there is no leading off but the baserun-

ner can leave the base as soon as the ball leaves the pitcher's hand.

Timing is critical to stealing a base. If you wait until you actually see the ball leave the pitcher's hand, you've already lost valuable time. One trick, which Colleen is demonstrating above, is to start with one foot behind the bag. As the pitcher reaches the highest point of the delivery, Colleen strides forward with her back leg, but her foot stays on the bag until the ball leaves the pitcher's hand. This helps her get a good jump off the bag.

● *The Slide*

On a close play, the baserunner will want to slide to avoid the tag. Sliding can also be used to avoid overrunning a base. Instead of slowing down, the runner slides to a stop. Players should plan their slides well in advance and commit. Beginning a slide late or deciding not to slide once the motion has begun are two ways to cause an injury.

The straight-in, or bent-leg, slide offers the runner the best chance to get right back up. Colleen demonstrates on these two pages. She begins her slide 10 to 12 feet from the base. She bends her knees to drop her hips and then extends one leg toward the bag while tucking the other leg under the opposite knee. She slides on the hip and upper part of the thigh and is careful to keep her arms up in the air.

TAKING THE FIELD

The excitement really begins when you take the field against another team. Parents and friends fill the stands or bring their lawn chairs. It's time for you to put together all the skills you've practiced and to remember the rules you've memorized.

When you're standing alone at home plate, it's easy to feel outnumbered by the fielders. But the real battle is between you and the pitcher. When you step into the batter's box, make the pitcher throw strikes. Don't swing at balls that whiz by your nose or skim past your shoelaces. Wait for your pitch. Keep your eye on the ball and try to make contact. When you take the field, it's important to keep in mind the two unwritten rules of softball: Work hard and have fun!

Positions

Softball requires that nine people take the field on defense. Six players play in the infield: pitcher, catcher, short-stop, first, second, and third base. The other three players cover their territory in the outfield either in rightfield, left-field, or centerfield. Since slow-pitch softball is a hitter's game, some leagues allow a 10th player as a short-fielder in the outfield.

Conduct on the Field

When you play softball, show more maturity than many major league baseball players do. Don't kick dirt or throw your glove, hat, or bat. Impressionable young children may be watching, and you are a role model.

Don't argue the call with the umpire. Feel free to discuss the ump's need for a stronger prescription quietly with your teammates. Ask your coach if you think there should be an appeal to the umpire.

Keep the chatter going continuously. Chatter serves many purposes. A prime use is to make sure everyone knows the count and where to make the throw. You can build up your teammates with phrases like "Nice pitch" and "Good throw." Or you can tease your opponents by yelling "Easy out" and "No batter." Just be prepared. Some players will respond to "She's afraid to take the bat off her shoulder!" by jacking the ball over the centerfielder's head. After all, that's what you'll do, right?

● *Pitcher*

A complete pitcher does more than face batters. Once a pitcher releases the ball, the job description changes. The pitcher becomes an infielder. One important duty is to **back up** the catcher on a play at home. Depending on the number and placement of runners on base, the pitcher may also back up a throw to second or third. An added responsibility in fast-pitch is covering the plate if a pitch gets away from the catcher. An aggressive baserunner on third might try to steal home.

● Catcher

Catchers need to be quick, tough, and flexible. They need thighs of steel since they spend much of their defensive time in either a crouch or a squat position. They have to be ready for pop flies, finger-stinging foul tips, and runners barreling down the third base line intent on knocking the ball loose on the tag.

Catchers lead the defense. They study the opposing batters for strengths and weaknesses. They take charge of the chatter and make sure everyone knows the count and number of outs. Experienced catchers will know when and how to take their pitcher aside for an encouraging word. They also know when it's time for their pitcher to be replaced.

Fast-pitch rules and techniques give the catcher extra responsibilities. The catcher decides which pitch should be thrown. To give the sign, Katie squats with her thighs resting on her calves, as in the bottom left photo. She sends a series of hand signals with her fingers pointing toward the dirt. Her legs screen her hand from the base coaches so that they can't tell what pitch will be thrown. Then she holds up her mitt to give the pitcher a target. Katie puts her bare hand behind her back to protect it.

Once a runner makes it onto the base paths, the catcher watches for the steal. After giving the sign, the catcher moves from the squat to the up position. The catcher's legs are bent at the knee almost as though he or she were sitting in a chair. The catcher bends forward and extends the mitt. While arm strength is important, quickness and accuracy play an important role in persuading runners to stay put.

When a runner is on base, the catcher's most important job is to make sure the ball doesn't get past him or her. If the pitcher throws the ball in the dirt, the catcher must block the ball by falling to the knees and putting the tip of the glove in the dirt. The catcher should lean forward so the ball won't bounce over a shoulder.

● *First Base*

Like Tamara, the person playing first is frequently tall. Those added inches can help when catching a high, wild throw. In slow-pitch, the defensive position is behind and to the left of the base. In fast-pitch, Tamara, above, plays in front of the base, near the baseline, to defend against the bunt.

On a well-thrown ball, Tamara places her bare-hand foot on the corner of the bag. She stretches as far as possible to reduce the distance that the ball needs to travel. Above all, she must catch the ball so a single doesn't turn into a double. When a throw from the shortstop is in the dirt at Tamara's feet, she puts the tip of her glove close to the ground so the ball won't roll under it. She keeps her eye on the ball until it rolls or bounces into her glove.

In the photos on this page, Molly is the shortstop. When the batter hits a pop fly in Molly's direction, she calls out that she'll catch it. Then, she runs to get underneath the ball while the leftfielder backs up the play.

● Second Base and Shortstop

Both infielders at second base and shortstop need superior fielding ability and throwing accuracy. In slow-pitch, shortstop is the most demanding position because most of the balls are hit to that area of the field. In fast-pitch, the possibility of a steal complicates the job at second base.

The good or bad plays made at second base can change the outcome of a game. After all, once a runner reaches second base, that runner is in **scoring position.** The players standing to either side of second must work closely together and know who is going to cover the base on every conceivable play.

In general, when the ball is hit toward the rightfield side of second, the shortstop will cover the base while the fielder at second plays the ball. If the ball is hit to the leftfield side of second, the fielder at second goes to the base while the shortstop fields the ball.

● *Third Base*

The third base position sees the greatest variety of balls—from slow rollers and bunts to red-hot liners, such as the one the fielder is fielding at right. The person at third needs a strong arm to throw out the runner at first base.

Frequently, a baserunner advances to third on an extra-base hit and must be tagged out. In the photos below, notice that Kathy doesn't stand between the runner and third base. Such a strategy could lead to an interference call or an injury. Instead, Kathy straddles the bag. She places her glove and the bare hand holding the ball down and in front of the base. She lets the runner slide into it.

Hitting the Cutoff

Usually, the shortstop or the fielder covering second base will take the cutoff to relay the ball to the infield. Relays are used when the throw is beyond the range of an outfielder or if it's important to get the ball to a base quickly. A ball can be returned to the infield more rapidly by two flat, short throws than by a single, high throw.

In the example shown above, a ball is hit to Colleen in centerfield. Molly, the shortstop, sees that a runner is headed for home. Molly races to a spot in a straight line between the centerfielder and the catcher. Colleen fires the ball to Molly so that it reaches her at chest level. Molly catches the ball. She pivots backward on her ball-hand foot and quickly relays the ball to Tripper with no wasted motion.

● *Outfield*

Outfielders must possess speed, fielding ability, and a good arm. The centerfielder needs the most speed since that territory is largest. The leftfielder needs to be prepared for hard shots down the third base line. The rightfielder must have a strong arm to throw the ball to third base.

When the pitcher and infielders seem to be making all the outs, outfielders can have a tough time concentrating. Outfielders can overcome this problem and tighten up their team's defense by backing up their teammates. Even when the ball doesn't make it into the outfield, the outfielders should know which base to back up on each play in case of a bad throw. For example, rightfielders can back up every throw to first base.

Another way to stay alert is for the outfielders to pay attention to each batter and adjust their position depending on whether the batter is right- or left-handed. They should also consider the batter's size, stance, and where he or she hit the ball the last time.

The Game

To give you an idea of how these skills are used in a game, we'll follow the Maroons and the Golds as these rivals enter the seventh and final inning of their game. The Maroons have six runs. The Golds have five. The game began with a show of offensive power on both sides. The first inning ended four runs to three. After that, both pitchers settled down into their rhythms, allowing only a few runners to move all the way around the bases.

Before the last inning starts, Katie catches Leah's final practice pitch and fires it to Allison at second base. Katie yells "Let's go! Three up. Three down."

The first Golds batter walks toward the plate. She takes two final practice swings before stepping into the batter's box. Leah gets the signal from Katie. Her arm rotates up and back in the windmill.

The ball slaps into Katie's mitt. The umpire says nothing. He lifts his left hand. The Golds in the dugout congratulate their teammate on her good eye. Leah catches the ball from Katie and ignores the noise to her right. She delivers another pitch. The Golds batter swings. The ball spins over the bat and high into the air. Katie rips the mask off her face so she can find the ball more easily. She spots it coming down to her right and tosses her mask to the left so she won't trip over it. Her bare hand follows the ball into her mitt. One out.

Dorothy, the next Golds batter, steps up to the plate. Katie signals a rise ball. Leah delivers it. Dorothy swings where she thought the ball would be—at chest level. The pitch whizzes past her shoul-

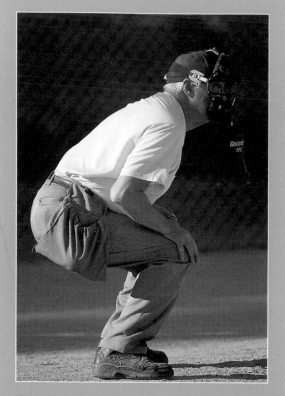

Behind the Plate

Umpires enforce the rules of the game. Like the catcher, the home plate umpire wears a face mask and chest protector. The home plate umpire calls balls and strikes and decides whether the ball is fair or foul. The base umpires rule on whether a batter is safe or out and whether an outfielder has caught a ball before it touched the ground. When there is only one umpire officiating, he or she will often run into the infield to get a closer look at the plays.

ders. "Strike!" the umpire announces. "Nice cut, Dorothy," the Golds coach calls from the first base coach's box. "Gotta have a strike next time."

On the next pitch, Dorothy drives a hard ground ball up the middle. The centerfielder charges the ball and sidearms it to Allison at second base. Dorothy rounds first base, but quickly retreats to the bag.

As Anne leaves the **on-deck circle**, the Maroons on first and third take a couple steps forward. Not only is it a sacrifice bunt situation, but Anne laid down a picture-perfect drag bunt for a single earlier in the game. As Leah begins her delivery, Anne shifts into the bunting stance facing the pitcher. The fielders at first and third charge toward the plate while Allison covers first base.

Anne directs the ball into the dirt up the third base line. The fielder playing third base allows the ball to dribble over the white chalk line. "Foul ball!" the umpire roars.

Anne walks back to the plate and picks up her bat. Leah burns in another inside pitch. Instead of bunting, Anne drives a blistering line drive up the third base line. The ball lands fair before curving into foul territory. Dorothy scores. The third base coach sends Anne home. Anne begins her slide several strides before the base. Her feet slide under the catcher's mitt. The umpire signals that she is safe.

Katie hands the ball to Leah, who had backed up the play at home. "Shake it off," Katie tells Leah. "Get the next two batters."

Leah maintains her composure. The next two Golds batters ground out to the shortstop. Katie dashes to the dugout to take off her chest protector and shin guards. She's at the top of the **batting order.**

"Start us off, Katie," Leah calls as she pulls a jacket onto her pitching arm. Katie grins at her friend from the on-deck circle before returning her attention to the Golds pitcher to study her rhythm. When Katie steps into the batter's box, she keeps her eyes fixed on the ball all the way in until she stares down the barrel of her bat. The ball flies over the backstop. "That wasn't your pitch, Katie," Molly calls from the Maroons' dugout.

The second pitch looks high and outside, but the umpire calls another strike. Katie stops herself from looking over her shoulder at the ump with disbelief. The groan of the fans behind the plate says it all. Katie steps out of the box and takes a practice swing.

Then Katie taps a blooper over the shortstop's head. The ball drops neatly into the hole between the infield and outfield for a single.

Mary follows her teammate's performance by driving one up the middle. Dorothy charges the ball. It takes an odd bounce over her glove. The ball bounces off Dorothy's leg and rolls several feet away. The leftfielder, who was backing up her teammate, makes the stop. The third base coach holds up Katie at third as Mary has a stand-up double.

The Golds pitcher walks the next batter, loading the bases. Then Leah steps up to the plate. She puts a hard fly ball into the hole between the rightfielder and centerfielder. The runner on first starts for second, confident that the ball won't be caught, but Dorothy makes a diving catch. She rolls to her feet and throws the ball to first base.

The ball beats the runner back to first. Two outs! But in the meantime, Katie tagged up at third on the fly ball and makes it home to tie the game.

Leah walks back to her dugout and finds a spot next to Katie on the bench. She stares at the pattern of dirt on her shoes. "Hey, don't look so down," Katie says. "That was a great hit." Leah slides one arm into her jacket. "Thanks. It's just that my arm is getting tired. I'm not sure if I can get another inning out of it."

Katie finishes strapping her shin guards around her legs. "Don't worry. Their pitcher is getting tired too, and we have Mary in scoring position."

Leah looks pointedly at Katie's shin guards. Katie follows her teammate's gaze and laughs. "I have to be ready, don't I?"

Leah and Katie leap to their feet as Mary goes to third on a **wild pitch**. The catcher dashes back to the backstop to get it. She hangs onto the ball since Mary's speed makes an out impossible. "Get a little hit, Diane," Molly calls as the next batter approaches the plate. "I want to go home."

Diane quickly gets two strikes against her. With nerves of steel, she lets the next two balls go by. Then she drives a hard liner between second and third. The person playing third leaps to make the catch. The ball bounces off the top of her glove into short leftfield. The leftfielder bare-hands the ball and fires it to first. Thud. Slap. Diane beats the throw by a split second. Mary scores. The Maroons win the game! Diane and Mary lead their team to the center of the field to shake hands with the other team.

SOFTBALL TALK

arc: The vertically curved path of a pitch to the plate.

back up: To get behind the fielder who is going to make the catch, in case the ball gets past him or her.

bad hop: An unexpected bounce of a thrown or batted ball.

ball: A pitch that doesn't pass through the strike zone and at which the batter doesn't swing.

batting order: The set order in which the team bats. Players may not bat out of order, but substitutions are allowed.

bunt: A softly hit ball.

changeup: An intentionally slow pitch that is thrown with the same motion as a fast pitch to fool the batter.

count: The number of balls and strikes against a batter. The number of balls is always given first. So if the umpire has called two strikes and the pitcher has also thrown three balls, the count is 3-and-2—three balls and two strikes.

curveball: A pitch that curves toward or away from a batter.

drag bunt: A bunt that a batter disguises until the last possible moment. A drag bunt is used when the batter is trying to reach base safely.

drop ball: A ball that moves sharply down as it approaches the plate.

extra-base hit: A hit that allows the batter to advance past first base. A *double* gets the batter to second base, a *triple* to third, and a *home run* to home plate.

fly ball: A ball that is hit high into the air in fair territory.

force-out: A situation in which a baserunner must go to the next base, but the fielder holding the ball touches the base before the runner. A force-out, also called a force play, can only happen at first base or when all the bases behind the runner are occupied.

foul ball: A batted ball that lands outside the foul lines.

ground ball: A batted ball that rolls on the ground. Also called a grounder.

line drive: A hard-hit ball that travels on a straight, relatively low path.

on-deck circle: The area, often outlined with chalk, where the next batter in the order waits.

opposite field: Rightfield for a righthanded batter and leftfield for a lefthanded batter.

out: The failure of a batter or runner to reach a base safely. A team is allowed three outs in an inning.

pitcher's rubber: The rectangle set in the middle of the infield where the pitcher must stand when delivering the ball.

pocket: The webbing of a glove between the thumb and forefinger.

pull the ball: Hitting the ball to leftfield for a righthanded batter and rightfield for a lefthanded batter.

rise ball: A pitch that moves upward sharply as it approaches the plate.

sacrifice bunt: A play in which the batter bunts and is put out but succeeds in moving a teammate at least one base. The batter's team must have fewer than two outs.

scoring position: A baserunner on second or third base is in scoring position.

strike: A pitch that passes through the strike zone without being hit. Also, a pitch that is hit foul when the batter has fewer than two strikes.

strikeout: An out that results from the batter being charged with three strikes.

strike zone: The invisible area over home plate through which the pitch must pass to be called a strike.

stuff: The adjusting of a pitch so that it drops, rises, or curves.

tag: An out a fielder makes by touching a runner with the ball.

tag up: The act of touching one's original base, after a fielder catches a fly ball, in order to be able to go to the next base.

walk: A free pass to first base, awarded to a batter who takes four balls without being put out by a strikeout or a fielder. Also called a base on balls.

wild pitch: A pitch well outside the strike zone that is difficult for the catcher to block or catch.

FURTHER READING

Dickson, Paul. *The Worth Book of Softball: A Celebration of America's True National Pastime.* New York: Facts on File, 1994.

Gutman, Bill. *Softball for Boys and Girls: Start Right and Play Well.* New York: Marshall Cavendish, 1990.

Kneer, Marian E. and Charles L. McCord. *Softball: Slow and Fast Pitch.* Dubuque, Iowa: Brown & Benchmark, 1995.

Potter, Diane L. *Softball: Steps to Success.* Champaign, Ill.: Human Kinetics Publishers, Inc., 1989.

Walker, Dick. *Softball: A Step-By-Step Guide.* Mahwah, N.J.: Troll Associates, 1990.

FOR MORE INFORMATION

Amateur Softball Association
2801 N.E. 50th Street
Oklahoma City, OK 73111

Cinderella Softball Leagues
P. O. Box 1411
Corning, NY 14830

INDEX